Options Trading Crash Course:

A Beginners's guide to investing and making profit with options trading + Day Trading Strategies + Swing Trading.

|2021 Edition|

TABLE OF CONTENTS

Legal & Disclaimer

The information contained in this book and its contents is not designed to replace or take the place of any form of medical or professional advice; and is not meant to replace the need for independent medical, financial, legal or other professional advice or services, as may be required. The content and information in this book have been provided for educational and entertainment purposes only.

The content and information contained in this book has been compiled from sources deemed reliable, and it is accurate to the best of the Author's knowledge, information and belief. However, the Author cannot guarantee its accuracy and validity and cannot be held liable for any errors and/or omissions. Further, changes are periodically made to this book as and when needed. Where appropriate and/or necessary, you must consult a professional (including but not limited to your doctor, attorney, financial advisor or such other professional advisor) before using any of the suggested remedies, techniques, or information in this book.

Upon using the contents and information contained in this book, you agree to hold harmless the Author from and against any damages, costs, and expenses, including any legal fees potentially resulting from the application of any of the information provided by this book. This disclaimer applies to any loss, damages or injury caused by the use and application, whether directly or indirectly, of any advice or information presented, whether for breach of contract, tort, negligence, personal injury, criminal intent, or under any other cause of action.

You agree to accept all risks of using the information presented inside this book.

You agree that by continuing to read this book, where appropriate and/or necessary, you shall consult a professional (including but not limited to your doctor, attorney, or financial advisor or such other advisor as needed) before using any of the suggested remedies, techniques, or information in this book.

Chapter 1

INTRODUCTION

An option trading is a way for skilled investors to leverage assets and control certain market risks. Most investors are acquainted with the words "buy low and sell high." However, options allow them to benefit from rising or falling stocks or from the side. With relatively small cash, you can take the options of reducing losses, protecting gains, and controlling large parts of the stock.

Optional strategies, on the other hand, can be difficult and risky. You could not only lose your full investment, but theoretically, some strategies can expose you to unlimited loss.

So, it is important to consider the effects that variables such as implied volatility and time decay have on your strategy before you take any trade options. You can answer these hard questions in this Playbook. Don't think about it; just turn to the strategy.

The Black Scholes option price model will not be derived here. Indeed, this is one of the only times the Black-Scholes model has been mentioned. It is nice to note some different things, but the aim here is to provide the basic knowledge needed to trade a specific strategy, not to completely bore the pants off of you.

Throughout this book, you'll also find "Options guide Tips," which clarify basic concepts or give you an additional advice on how to run a particular strategy. There's a little picture of my head next to them as an indicator of the importance of these tips like that you see on the right side. Therefore, be sure to take extra concentration.

Many good options traders know nothing about the following historical facts. But for those inquisitive souls, we have included this section to learn all possible information on whatever subject they choose to study.

1.1 A brief history of option trading

Options are currently often successfully used as a tool for speculation and risk reduction. However, the market for options did not always work as smoothly as today. Let's begin with a look at the debacle of 17th century Holland, commonly referred to as the "Tulip Bulb Mania."

Tulips were very popular among Dutch aristocrats as a status symbol in the early 1600s. And as the popularity of the companies began to spill over to a worldwide market across Holland, prices were dramatically increasing.

Tulip wholesalers began to purchase call options, and tulip growers began to protect their earnings with put options, in order to protect the Risk of poor harvest.

In Holland, options trading first appear to be an entirely reasonable business. But the value of existing options contracts increased dramatically as the prices for tulip bulbs continued to rise. Thus, the general public emerged as a secondary market for these options contracts. In fact, family members could use their whole fortune to speculate on the market of tulip bulbs.

Sadly, the bubble erupted, and the price of tulips plummeted when the Dutch economy slowed down in 1638. Many of the speculators who sold options could not meet their obligations. The options market in Holland in the 17th century was totally unregulated; this makes matters worse. Therefore you could not obtain blood from a stone despite the efforts of the Netherlands Government to force speculators to do better on their options contracts. thousands of ordinary Hollanders lost more than their frilly-collared shirts. (Thus, a dried, dried up tulip bulb, for the matter). At this time, options managed were acquiring a bad reputation, which made it last for almost two to three centuries.

1.2 Where we stand today

The development of computerized trading systems and the Internet has created a market for far more viable and liquid options. We saw several new players entering the marketplace because of this. As of this date, Boston Bursary, Chicago Bureau, International Securities Exchange, NASDAQ OMX PHLX, NASDAQ Stock Market, NYSE AMEX, and NYSE Arca have been included on the options exchanges listed in the United States.

So today, for any investor (especially with Ally Invest), it is remarkably easy to place an optional trade. The average number of option contracts traded on over 3,000 securities is over 11 million every day the market still continues to grow. And thanks to the wide range of book resources (such as the book you read at the moment), the public knows better than ever before about options.

The most important event in the history of options was the introduction of Ally Invest to the investment public in December 2005. Indeed, it has been in our modest opinion, with the possible exception of the Big Bang and a cozy invention, the most important event in the history of the universe. But those last two we're not sure.

Chapter 2

HOW OPTION PRICE ARE DETERMINED

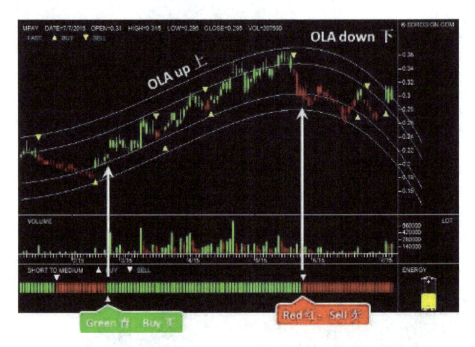

Options are contracts that enable option buyers to buy or sell a security on or before a fixed day at a predetermined price. There are a number of numerious variables in the price of an option known as premium. Options traders must be aware of these variables so that they can decide in an informed way when to trade an option.

Options are broken down into options "call" and "put" The contract buyer acquires the right, with a call option, and to buy the underlying asset at a predetermined price, known as the exercise price or strike price, in the future. By means of a put option, the buyer shall be entitled to the future to sell the basic asset at the default rate.

However, the profitability of an option agreement is also affected by many other factors. Some such factors include the price or premium for the stock option, how long it remains for the expiry of the contract, and how much the safety or stock underlying the value changes.

2.1 Factors That Determine Option Pricing

Options can really be used in a wide range, from conservative to high-risk strategies. They can also be used to meet expectations beyond simple guidelines. Therefore, once you learn terminology for basic options, it makes sense to examine factors in different scenarios that affect the cost of an option.

• Options are derivative contracts with the right to buy or sell some assets at a pre-defined price on or before the contract ends, but not with the obligation.

• Options may be used for directional strategies or to cover certain market risks.

The price of an option depends on complex mathematical formulas, but the prices of the underlying assets are the price, the option strike, time to expiry, interest rates, and the implicated volatility of the Option.

When stock traders begin to use options first, they usually buy a call or a directional trading arrangement in which they expect that the stock moves in a specific direction. These traders can select an option instead of the stock because of the limited Risk, high reward, and less capital needed to control the same number of shares.

If the perspective is good (bullish), a call option creates the opportunity to share the upside potential without risking more than a fraction of the market value. When bizarre, the buyer can benefit from a drop without the necessary margin to sell shorts

The Option can be utilized in a number of strategies, from traditional to Risk, which is high. They could additionally be customized to meet expectations that go beyond simple directional methods. Thus, when you learn simple Option terminology, it is practical to investigate variables affecting an option's cost in numerous scenarios.

2.2 The Key elements

• Options are derivative contracts the best, although not the obligation, to purchase (for a call option) or even sell-off (for a put option) some advantage in a predetermined cost on or perhaps prior to the contract expire.

• Options could be utilized for directional strategies or even to hedge against some risks on the market.

• Pricing a function depends on complicated mathematical formulas, though the immediate inputs to an option's price are the cost of the underlying asset, the Option's strike, moment to expiration, interest rates, and also implied volatility.

2.3 Utilizing Choices for Directional Strategies

When stock traders very first begin to use Option, it's typically to buy a put or a call for directional Trading, where they want a stock will go in a specific path. These traders may choose an Option instead of the underlying stock because of Risk that is limited, high reward potential as well as less capital required to manage the exact same number of shares.

In case the view is good (bullish), purchasing a call choice creates the chance to talk about the upside potential without needing to risk greater than a portion of the market value. When bearish, purchasing a put lets the trader use a fall without the margin necessary to sell short. Industry Direction and Value

Numerous kinds of option strategies could be constructed through the position's success, or maybe failure depends on a comprehensive understanding of the two types of options: the call and the put. Moreover, taking full advantage of choices involves a completely new means of contemplating because traders that believe exclusively in the terminology of industry direction miss all kinds of options.

Along with moving up or perhaps down, stocks are able to go sideways or trend lower or higher modestly for extended periods of time. They could additionally create sizable movements up and down in price, and then reverse direction and end up back exactly where they began. These types of cost movements result in headaches for inventory traders but offer Option traders the exclusive chance to generate cash even when the stock goes not. Calendar spreads, straddles, strangles butterflies spotlight a couple of Option methods created to make money in those kinds of cases.

Fundamentals of Option Pricing Option traders have to learn extra variables affecting an option's value as well as the intricacy of selecting the proper approach. When an inventory trader becomes great at predicting the future priced movement, he or maybe she might think it's a simple transition from choices, but this is not correct. Choices traders must deal with three shifting parameters which affect the cost: the cost of the underlying security, volatility, and time. Modifications in any or even most of these variables impact the Option's price.

Alternative pricing principle applies variables (stock price, interest rate, volatility, exercise price, the time it takes to expiration) to hypothetically appreciate an alternative. Basically, it offers an evaluation of an option's reasonable value that traders incorporate into the strategies of theirs to maximize profits. Some widely used models to value choices are Black-Scholes, Monte-Carlo simulation, and binomial option pricing. These theories have vast margins for error as a result of deriving the values of theirs from various other properties, normally the cost of a company's common stock. You will find mathematical formulas created to compute the reasonable value of an alternative. The trader just inputs known variables and receives a response that describes exactly what the alternative must be worth.

The main objective of every Option pricing model is calculating the likelihood that an Option is going to be worked out, or perhaps be in-the-money (ITM), at expiration. Underlying advantage cost (stock price), exercise price, volatility, interest rate, and time to expiration, and that is the number of days or weeks in between the formula day as well as the Option's exercise day, are usually utilized variables which are feedback into mathematical versions to gain an option 's theoretical reasonable worth.

2.4 Major Pricing Inputs

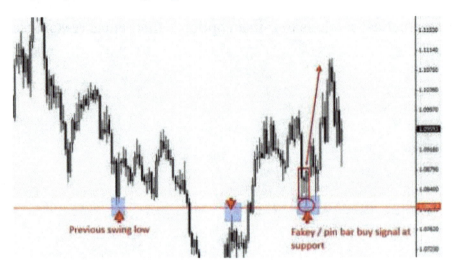

Let share the basic consequences which variables have on an option's price:

1. Underlying Price & Strike Price

The importance of calls and puts are impacted by changes in the underlying stock cost in a somewhat straightforward fashion. If the stock price goes up, calls must acquire in value since you're competent to purchase the underlying asset generally at a lower cost than the place that the industry is, and also places must lessen. Furthermore, put alternatives must improve in value and calls should decrease when the stock price tag declines, as the put holder provides the best to promote inventory at costs above the falling market cost.

That predetermined cost at what to purchase or maybe promote is known as the Option's strike price or even training selling price. Whenever the strike price tag permits you to purchase or even promote the underlying at a level that provides for a quick revenue purchase getting rid of that transaction in the open market, the Option is in-the-money (for instance a call to purchase shares at $10 if the market price tag is now $15, you are able to create a quick $5 earnings).

2. Time to Expiration

The result of time is very easy to conceptualize but takes knowledge before understanding the impact of its because of the expiration date. Time operates in the stock trader's favor, as great businesses often increase over extended time periods. Though time is definitely the enemy of the customer of options because, when days pass without a substantial change in the cost of the underlying, the valuation of the Option will drop. Additionally, the valuation of an Option is going to decline faster as it approaches the expiration date. Alternatively, that's news that is good for the Option seller, who attempts to make use of time decay, particularly throughout the last month, when it happens most quickly.

3. Interest Rates

Like the majority of any other financial assets, alternative costs are affected by prevailing interest rates and therefore are influenced by interest rate changes. Call choice and also place choice premiums are influenced inversely as interest rates change: calls benefit from growing prices while puts lose worth. The Option holds true when interest rates fall.

4. Volatility

The result of volatility on an option 's value may be the hardest idea for newbies to realize. It depends on a measure known as statistical (sometimes called historical) volatility, or maybe SV for the brief, taking a look at previous cost moves of the inventory with a certain time period.

Option pricing models need the trader to enter upcoming volatility during the lifetime of the possibility. Obviously, choice traders do not truly understand what it is going to be as well as must imagine by operating the pricing model "backward." All things considered, the trader probably knows the cost at that the choice is Trading and will investigate various other variables like time, dividends, and interest rates left with a little bit of investigation. As an outcome, the one missing quantity is going to be upcoming volatility, which could be believed from various other inputs

The inputs from the center of implied volatility, is a crucial measure utilized by options traders. It's known as implied volatility (IV) since it enables traders to find out what they believe potential volatility is apt to be.

Traders utilize IV to gauge whether Option is expensive or cheap. You might listen to choice traders state that premium levels are high or maybe that premium levels are reduced. What they truly mean would be that the current IV is low or high. When understood, the trader is able to determine when it's a great time to buy Options - since premiums are inexpensive - when it's a great time to sell Option - because they're costly.

Sell Trade Example: AUD/USD (Australian Dollar / US Dollar), M15 Chart

Buy Trade Example: AUD/USD (Australian Dollar / US Dollar), M15 Chart

Chapter 3

FUNDAMENTAL OPTIONS STRATEGIES GOING LONG

Options are conditional derivative contracts which enable buyers of the contracts (option holders) to purchase or even promote security in a selected value. Choice buyers are charged an amount referred to as a "premium" by the sellers for such a perfect. Must market rates be unfavorable for selection holders; they are going to let the choice expire worthlessly, and therefore ensuring the losses aren't higher compared to the premium. In comparison,

Option sellers (Option writers) assume greater danger compared to the possible buyers, which is the reason they expect this premium.

Options are split into "put" and "call" options. With a call option, the customer of the agreement purchases the right to purchase the underlying asset in the world in a predetermined price tag, called exercise cost, or maybe hit selling price. With a put option, the customer acquires the proper to market the underlying asset in the world at the fixed price tag.

Traders frequently go into trading options with very little knowledge of options methods. There are lots of tactics offered that limit danger and maximize return. With a bit of effort, traders are able to discover the right way to make use of the flexibility as well as power options offer. With this in mind, we have come up with this primer, which might reduce the learning curve as well as use you in the correct path.

3.1 10 Options Strategies to know.

1 Covered Call

With calls, one method is in order to purchase a naked call choice. You are able to likewise design a fundamental covered call or buy-write. This is an extremely popular strategy since it creates income and reduces some danger of becoming a lengthy inventory alone. The trade-off is the fact that you

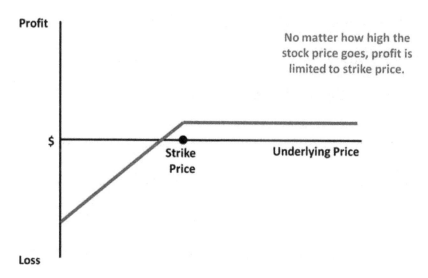

should be prepared to promote the shares of yours at a set price: the brief strike selling price. In order to perform the technique, you buy the basic stock as you usually would, and concurrently create (or sell) a call option on all those same shares.

In this particular illustration, we're utilizing a call choice on a stock, which represents a hundred shares of stock every call choice. For every hundred shares of stock you purchase, you simultaneously sell one call choice against it. It's described as a covered call since in the function that a stock rockets much higher in cost, the short call of yours is protected by the very long inventory job. Investors may use this strategy when they have a short-term placement in the stock, along with a neutral opinion on the direction of its. They may be trying to produce money (through the purchase of the call premium), and guard against a possible drop in the basic stock's worth.

Notice just how, as the stock price increases, the negative P&L from the call is set off by the very long shares job. Simply because you get high quality from offering the call, as the inventory moves throughout the strike price on the benefit, the high quality you got lets you efficiently market the stock of yours in a greater amount compared to the strike cost (strike + premium received). The covered call 's P&L graph looks a great deal like a very short naked put's P&L graph.

2. Married Put

In a married put approach, an investor buys an asset (in this particular illustration, shares of stock), and concurrently purchases put choices for an equivalent amount of shares. The holder of a put choice has got the best to promote inventory in the strike price. Each contract may be worth a hundred shares. The main reason and investor would utilize this method is in order to protect their downside danger when having a stock. This strategy functions the same as an insurance policy and also establishes a cost floor when the stock's value falls sharply.

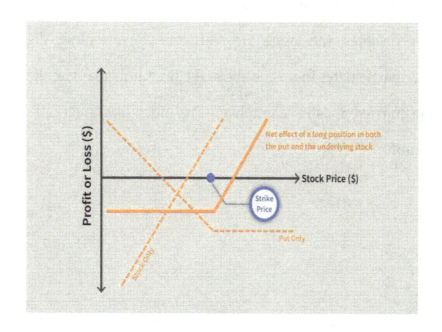

A good example of a married put will be whether an investor purchases a hundred shares of stock and purchases one put

option concurrently. This particular method is appealing since an investor is shielded to the disadvantage must a bad event occur. At exactly the same period, the investor would take part in the benefit in case of the stock profits in worth. The sole drawback of this approach happens if the stock doesn't fall; in that case, the investor will lose the premium spent on the put option.

In the P& L graph earlier, the dashed line stands out as the long inventory job. Together with the long put as well as night stock positions combined, you are able to realize that when the stock price tag declines, the losses are restricted. Nevertheless, the inventory participates in upside above the premium spent on the put. The married put's P& L graph appears much like much call's P&; L graph.

3. Bull Call Spread

In this the bull call spread strategy, an investor will concurrently purchase phone calls in a certain hit cost and promote the exact same amount of phone calls at a greater hit selling price. Both call Option is going to have the very same expiration and underlying advantage. This particular kind of vertical spread tactic is commonly utilized when an investor is bullish on the basic as well as expects a reasonable increase in the cost of the advantage. The investor restricts his/her upside on the industry but decreases the total premium invested when compared with purchasing a naked phone call Option outright.

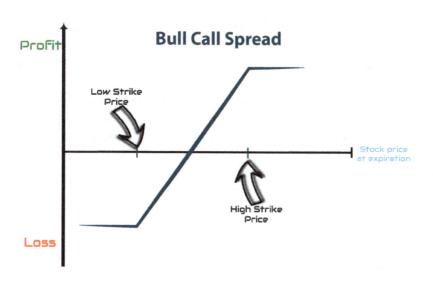

In the P&L graph earlier, you are able to realize that this is a bullish approach. Therefore the trader requires the stock to rise in cost to be able to create an income on the industry. The trade-off, when putting holding a bull call spread, is the fact that the upside of yours is restricted, while your premium invested is reduced. When outright calls are very pricey, a proven way to counterbalance the bigger premium is by promoting greater strike calls against them. This's the way a bull call spread is built.

4. Bear Put Spread

The bear placed spread plan is yet another kind of vertical spread. In this particular technique, the investor will concurrently buy put alternatives in a certain hit cost and promote the exact same amount of places at a lower hit selling price. Both alternatives will be for similar underlying assets and also have exactly the same expiration date. This particular method is needed once the trader is bearish and expects the underlying asset's cost to drop. It provides both limited losses in addition to limited gains.

In the PL graph earlier, you are able to realize that this is a bearish approach; therefore, you want the stock to fall to be able to make money. The trade-off, when employing a bear put spread is the fact that the upside of yours is restricted; however, your premium invested is reduced. When outright places are very pricey, a proven way to counterbalance the excessive premium is by promoting reduced strike throws against them. This is the way a bear put spread is built.

5. Protective Collar

A defensive collar tactic is performed by buying an out-of-the-money put feature and concurrently writing an out-of-the-money call option for the same underlying expiration and asset. This particular method is commonly utilized by investors after an extended position in a stock has encountered sizable gains. This particular alternative mixture enables investors to have downside protection (long places to secure in profits) while keeping the trade-off of possibly being required to offer shares at a greater cost (selling greater = more benefit than at existing stock levels).

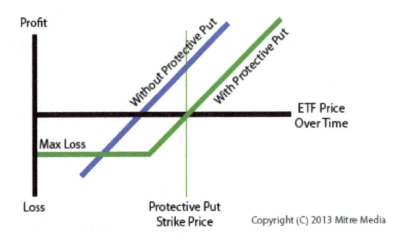

A basic case in point is whether an investor is extended a hundred shares of IBM for $50, and IBM has risen to $100 as of January 1st. The investor could create a defensive collar by selling 1 IBM March 15th hundred five calls and concurrently purchasing one IBM March $90 puts. The trader is shielded under $95 until

March 15th, with the trade-off of possibly keeping the obligation to promote his/her shares at $100

In the P& L graph earlier, you are able to realize that the defensive collar is a blend associated with a covered call and much put. This is a basic trade set up, indicating you're shielded in the event of dropping inventory, but with the trade-off of getting the possible obligation to market the long stock of yours in the quite short call strike. Once again, however, the investor must be pleased to do, and so, as they've previously encountered gains in the main shares.

6. Long Straddle

A very long straddle choices tactic happens when an investor simultaneously buys a call and put choice on a similar underlying asset, with exactly the same hit cost as well as an expiration date. An investor will frequently make use of this technique as he or maybe she thinks the cost of the underlying asset will shift considerably from a stove but is uncertain of what direction the move usually takes. This particular plan enables the investor to have the chance for theoretically

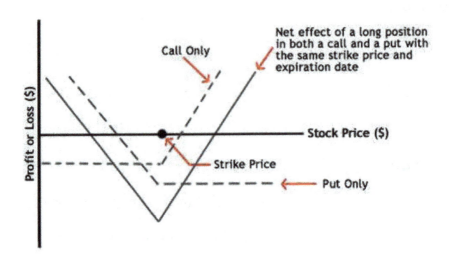

Limitless gains, even though the maximum loss is restricted just to the price of both choices contracts combined.

In the P& L graph earlier, notice just how you will find two breakeven points. This particular strategy becomes lucrative whenever the stock makes a big move of one direction or the other person. The investor does not care what direction the stock movements, just it's a much better action compared to the entire premium the investor spent on the structure.

7. Long Strangle

In much strangle options technique, the investor purchases an out-of-the-money call feature as well as an out-of-the-money put option at the same time on identical underlying advantage as well as an expiration date. An investor that utilizes this particular plan thinks the underlying asset's cost is going to experience an extremely big movement but is uncertain of what direction the move usually takes.

This may, for instance, become a wager on an earnings release for a business or maybe an FDA function for a healthcare inventory. Losses are restricted to the costs (or premium spent) for both choices. Strangles will usually be more affordable than straddles because the choices bought are out of the investment.

In the P&L graph earlier, notice just how you will find two breakeven points. This particular strategy becomes lucrative whenever the stock makes a really big move in one direction or even the other person. Once again, the investor does not care what direction the stock movements, just it's a much better action compared to the entire premium the investor spent on the structure.

8. Long Call Butterfly Spread

Every one of the techniques up to this point has demanded a mix of 2 various jobs or even contracts. In much butterfly spread utilizing call option, an investor is going to combine both a bull spread program as well as a bear spread program, and also utilize three distinct strike rates. All choices are for the same underlying advantage as well as an expiration date.

Long Butterfly

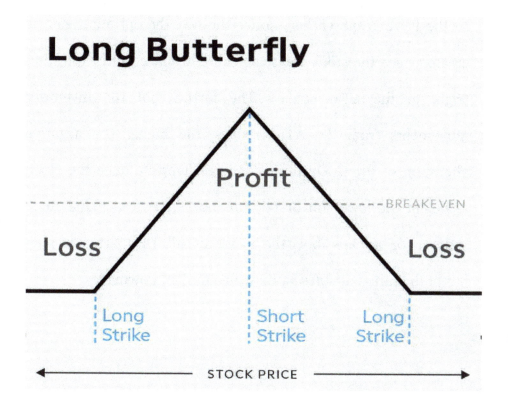

For instance, much butterfly spread may be built by buying one in-the-money call option in a lower hit price, while selling two at-the-money call option, and purchasing one out-of-the-money call option. A healthy butterfly spread is going to have the very same wing widths. This particular instance is known as a "call fly," as well as results in a total debit. An investor would enter right into much butterfly call spread whenever they believe the stock won't move very much by expiration.

In the P& L graph earlier, notice the way the optimum gain is created once the stock stays the same in place until expiration (right at the ATM strike). The further out the inventory movements from the ATM strikes, the higher the negative alteration of P& L. Optimum damage happens once the stock settles at the lower hit or perhaps below, or even if the stock settles at or perhaps above the bigger hit call. This particular plan has both limited upsides along with a limited downside.

9. Iron Condor

An even more fascinating strategy will be the iron condor. In this particular technique, the investor simultaneously keeps a bull put spread along with a bear call spread. The iron condor is built by offering one out-of-the-money put and purchasing one out-of-the-money put associated with a reduced hit (bull put spread), plus promoting one out-of-the-money call and purchasing one out-of-the-money call of a greater hit (bear call spread). All choices have exactly the same expiration date and are on a similar underlying asset. Generally, the put, as well as call sides, have exactly the same spread width. This particular trading tactic earns a total premium on the structure, and it is created to make use of a stock experiencing very low volatility. A lot of traders this way trade because of its perceived high probability of making a tiny amount of premium.

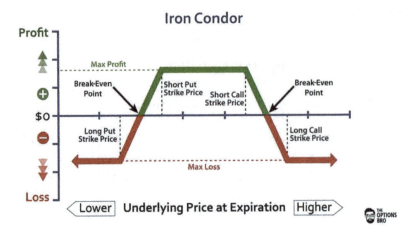

Iron Condor

In the P& L graph earlier, notice the way the optimum gain is created once the stock stays in a somewhat great trading range, which could lead to the investor making the entire net credit received when producing the trade. The further out the inventory moves from the short strikes (lower for the put, bigger for the call), the higher the damage up with the optimum loss. Optimum damage is normally considerably greater compared to the maximum gain, which intuitively makes good sense, given that there's a greater likelihood of the framework finishing with a little gain.

10. Metal Butterfly

The last option strategy we'll demonstrate will be the iron butterfly. In this particular technique, an investor is going to sell an at-the-money put and purchase an out-of-the-money put, while simultaneously offering an at-the-money call and purchasing an out-of-the-money phone call. All choices have exactly the same expiration date and are on a similar underlying asset. Although much like a butterfly spread, this particular approach differs since it utilizes both calls & puts instead of one or the other person.

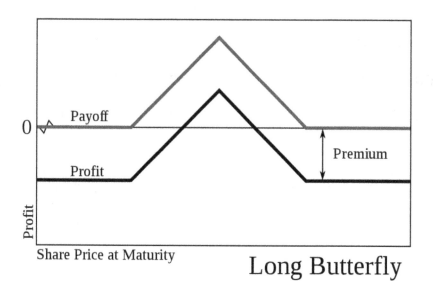

Long Butterfly

This particular method basically combines promoting an at-the-money straddle and purchasing shielding "wings." You are able to additionally think of the building as two spreads. It's typical to possess the very same width for equally spreads. The very long out-of-the-money call protects against the limitless downside. The very long out-of-the-money put protects against downside from the quite short put hit to zero. Profit, as well as loss, is both restricted within a certain range based on the strike costs of the choices utilized. Investors this way technique for the income it creates as well as the higher likelihood of a tiny grain with a non-volatile stock.

In the P& L graph earlier, notice the way the optimum gain is created once the stock stays at the at-the-money attacks of the call and put offered. The optimum gain is the complete net premium received. Optimum damage happens once the stock movements above the very long call strike and under the very long put strike.

Chapter 4

STRADDLE AS WELL AS STRANGLE

Straddles, as well as strangles, are both option methods that permit an investor to gain from substantial movements in a stock's value if the stock moves up or even down. Both solutions consist of purchasing an equal amount of call and put options that have the same expiration date. The difference would be that strangle has two distinct strike prices, even though the straddle has a typical strike price.

Options are a kind of derivative security, which means the cost of the Option is intrinsically connected to the expense of anything different. If perhaps you purchase an options contract, you have the proper, although not the obligation to purchase and promote an underlying advantage in a set price on or perhaps prior to a certain date.

A call option guide an investor with the best to purchase inventory, along with a put option, gives an investor the right to market stock. The strike cost of an option agreement will be the cost at what an underlying stock is purchased and sold. The stock should rise above this cost for falls or calls below for puts prior to a place that may be exercised for an income.

4.1 Key elements

• Straddles, as well as strangles, are option techniques investors' work with to gain from substantial movements in a stock's value, no matter the course.

• Straddles are helpful when it is not clear what direction the stock price may well go in, therefore in that way, the investor is protected, no matter the result.

• Strangles is helpful if the investor believes it is very likely the stock is going to move one of the ways or even another but would like to be protected in the event.

• Investors really should discover the complicated tax laws around how you can account for choices trading gains as well as losses.

4.2 Straddle

The straddle trade is a great strategy for a trader to make money on the price action of an underlying asset. Let us say business is scheduled to release the latest earnings results of its in 3 weeks' time, though you've no clue whether the news is going to be bad or good. These days prior to the news release will be a great moment to enter into a straddle as whenever the outcomes are released, the stock is apt to move lower or higher sharply.

Let us believe the stock is trading at $50 in the month of April. Suppose a $50 call option for June has a cost of $2two, even though the cost of the $50 put option for June is $1. A straddle is attained by purchasing both the put and the call for a total of $1: (two dollars + one dollar) x hundred shares a selection contract = $300.

The straddle increases in value in case the stock moves higher (because of the very long call option) and if the stock moves reduced (because of the long put option). Profits will be realized so long as the cost of the stock movements by over three dollars per share in both directions.

4.3 Strangle

Another method of Option is a strangle job. While a straddle doesn't have a directional bias, a strangle is utilized once the investor thinks the stock has a much better possibility of going in a particular path but would continue to love to be protected in the situation of a bad action.

For instance, Let's say you think a company 's results are going to be positive, which means you need less downside protection. Rather than purchasing the place option with the strike price of $50 for $1, perhaps you glance at purchasing the $ 12.50 strike, which has a cost of $0.25. This particular trade will be less expensive than the straddle as well as need much less of an upward action for you to break much.

Using the lower strike put option in this particular strangle will continue to protect you against the severe downside, while simultaneously placing you in a much better position to gain from a good announcement.

4.4 Exclusive Considerations

Understanding what taxes should be paid on options is definitely complicated, so any investor making use of these strategies needs to be acquainted with the laws for reporting losses and gains.

Irs Pub. 550: Capital Gains & Losses: Straddles offers an overview. Particularly, investors are going to want to check out the guidance about "offsetting positions" that the federal government describes as a "position which considerably reduces some danger of loss you might have from holding an additional position."

At some point on time, several options traders would adjust tax loopholes to postpone spending capital gains taxes - a method don't permit. Earlier, traders will enter offsetting positions and shut out the losing side by the conclusion of the entire year to gain from reporting a tax loss; concurrently, they'd allow the winning aspect of the industry remain open until the following season, thus stalling having to pay fees on virtually any gains.

Since tax rules are complicated, any investors offering in choices need to use tax experts that realize the complex laws set up.

Present "loss deferral rules" of Pub. 550 points out that a person can deduct a loss on a place and then the degree that the loss is much more than any unrecognized gain the individual has available on offsetting positions. Any "unused losses are viewed as sustained in the following tax year."

There are far more regulations regarding offsetting positions, they're complicated, and also at times, it is not consistently applied. Options traders also need to consider the regulations for wash sale loss deferral, which would apply to traders who use saddles and strangles as well.

Rules are put in place by the Irs - as reported in Irs Pub. 550: Capital Gains and Losses: Wash Sales - to discourage investors from attempting to carry a tax deduction from a trade purchased in a clothes sale.

The wash sale happens when an individual offers or maybe trades at a loss. After that, both thirty times before or maybe after the transaction buys a "substantially identical" security or stock, and purchases a contract or perhaps Option to purchase the stock or perhaps protection. Awash sale additionally occurs when a person offers a holding, after which the spouse or maybe a business run by the person purchases a "substantially identical" security or stock.

Chapter 5

CREDIT SPREAD AND DEBIT SPREAD

When Trading or perhaps investing in choices, you can find many choice spread methods which one might use - a spread becoming the investment as well as the sale of various choices on a single root as a deal.

While we can classify spreads in different ways, one typical dimension is asking whether or maybe not the plan is a credit spread or even a debit spread. Credit spreads, and total credit spreads, are distributed tactics which involve total receipts of premiums, while debit spreads include total payments of premiums.

5.1 Key elements

• An alternatives spread is a method that entails the simultaneous buying as well as selling of choices on a similar underlying asset.

• A credit spread entails promoting a high premium choice while buying a low premium choice in the same category or of the same security, leading to a credit on the trader's account.

• A debit spread entails buying a high premium choice while offering a low premium choice in the same category and of the same protection, leading to debit from the trader's account.

5.2 credit Spreads

A credit spread consists of selling, or maybe writing, a high premium choice and simultaneously purchasing a lower premium choice. The premium got from the written choice is higher compared to the premium settled for the long choice, leading to a high quality credited into the trader or maybe investor's account whenever the position is opened. When traders or investors utilize a credit spread program, the maximum revenue they get will be the total premium. The credit spread leads to an income once the options' spreads narrow.

For instance, a trader tools a credit spread program by composing the 1st March call option with a strike price of $30 for $3 plus concurrently purchasing the 1st March call option with $40 for $1.

Since the typical multiplier on an equity choice is a hundred, the web premium received is $200 because of the swap. Moreover, the trader is going to profit when the spread tactic narrows.

A bearish trader expects stock prices to reduce, therefore, and, buys call choices (long call) in a particular hit cost and also offers (short call) the same amount of call options inside the same category along with the same expiration in a reduced hit selling price. In comparison, bullish traders expect stock prices to increase, and consequently, purchase call options in a particular hit cost and promote the same amount of call options inside the same category along with the same expiration in a greater hit selling price.

5.3 Debit Spreads

Alternatively, a debit spread - usually utilized by beginners to option techniques - requires purchasing an option with a greater premium and concurrently selling an alternative with a reduced premium, the place that the premium settled for the lengthy choice of the spread is much more than the premium gotten from the written choice.

Compared with a credit spread, a debit spread leads to a high quality debited, or maybe given, out of the trader's or perhaps investor's account whenever the position is opened. Debit spreads are largely used to offset the expenses related to owning long features positions.

For instance, a trader buys one could place choice with a strike price of $20 for $5 and also instantly sells one could put Option with a strike price of $10for $1. Thus, he paid $4 and $400for the swap. in case the trade is from the money, the max loss of his is lowered to $400, instead of $500 in case he just

Chapter 6

IRON CONDOR WHAT'S AN IRON CONDOR?

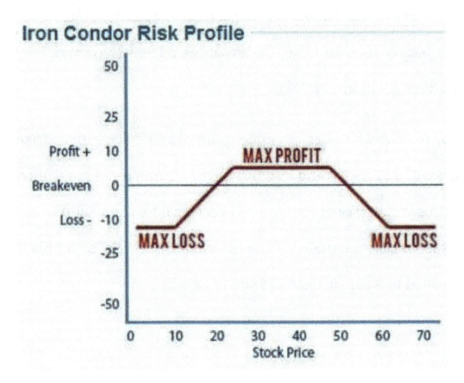

Iron Condor Risk Profile

An iron condor happens to be an option approach made up of 4 options comprising of 2 places (a long and one) that is short as well as two calls (one long and one short), along with four strike costs, most with the same expiration date. The aim is usually to profit from the low volatility of the underlying asset. Put simply; the iron condor earns the optimum revenue once the underlying asset closes in between the center hit rates at expiration.

The iron condor has an equivalent payoff as a typical condor spread but uses calls and put rather than just calls or even just puts. Both the condor along with the iron condor are extensions of the butterfly spread as well as iron butterfly, respectively.

6.1 Key elements

• An iron condor is usually a neutral approach as well as income most when the underlying asset does not move very much, although the technique could be designed with a bearish or bullish bias.

• The iron condor is made up of 4 options: a purchased place additional OTM and a sold put closer to the cash, along with a bought call further OTM and a sold call closer to the cash.

• Profit is capped at the premium gotten even though the threat is capped at the big difference in between the purchased as well as sold call hits as well as the bought and sold put strikes (less the premium received).

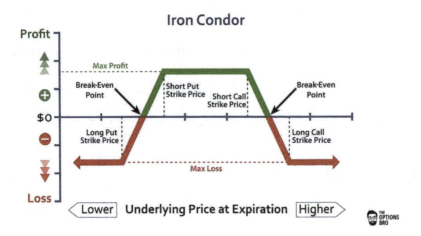

6.2 You need to understand the Iron Condor.

The method has restricted upside and downside danger as the low and high strike choices, the wings, guard against substantial movements in one or the other direction. Due to this minimal Risk, the profit potential of it is limited. The commission is usually a notable component here because there are four choices concerned.

Because of this technique, the trader preferably wants the alternatives to expire worthlessly, and that is just likely if the underlying asset closes in between the center two-hit rates at expiration. There'll probably be a charge to close the trade in case it's successful. When it's not profitable, the damage is still limited.

A good way to think of an iron condor is running much strangle interior of a bigger, short strangle (or maybe vice versa).

6.3 The building of the approach can be as follows:

1. Buy one from the cash (OTM) place with a strike cost below the present cost of the underlying asset. The out of the cash put alternative is going to protect against a major downside move on the underlying asset.

2. Sell one OTM and in cash (ATM) place with a strike priced closer to the present cost of the underlying asset.

3. Sell one ATM or OTM call with a strike cost above the present cost of the underlying asset.

4. Buy one OTM call with a strike cost more above the present cost of the underlying asset. The out of the cash call alternative is going to protect against a sizable upside move.

The choices which might be more from the cash, known as the wings, are both rather long positions. Due to the fact, these Options are more from the cash, the premiums of theirs are less than the two created Options, so there's a net recognition to the account when putting the trade.

By choosing various strike costs, it's doable to create the technique lean bullish or even bearish. For instance, if the center hit costs are above the present cost of the underlying asset, the trader hopes for a small increase in the price of its by expiration. It still has restricted reward along with the limited Risk.

6.4 Iron Condor Profits as well as Losses

The optimum benefit for an iron condor would be the quantity of premium, or maybe credit, received for producing the job of the four-leg choice.

The optimum loss is capped. The optimum loss is the big difference between the very long call as well as brief call strikes, or maybe the long put as well as brief put strikes. Reduce the loss by websites credits received; however, add commissions to obtain- Positive Many Meanings - the entire loss for the swap.

The greatest damage happens if the cost moves above the very long call strike (which is above the offered call strike) and under the very long put hit (which is less than the sold place hit).

Model of an Iron Condor on a Stock Believe that an investor thinks Apple Inc. (AAPL) is going to be fairly flat in the terminology of cost with the following two weeks. They opt to apply for an iron condor. The stock is now trading at $212.26

They offer a call with a $215 hit, giving them $ 7.63 in premium. They get a call with a strike of $ 220, which costs them $ 5.35. The recognition on these two legs is $ 2.28, or perhaps $ 228 for a single agreement (hundred shares). The trade is just half complete, however.

Additionally, the trader offers a put with a strike of $ 210, causing a premium gotten of $ 7.20. Additionally, they purchase a put with a strike of $ 205, costing $5.52. The total recognition on these two legs is $ 1.68 or perhaps $ 168 if trading one contract on each.

The entire recognition for the position is $ 3.96 ($ 2.28 + $ 1.68), or perhaps $396. This's the maximum revenue the trader can make. This particular highest benefit happens when all of the choices expire worthless, which suggests the purchase price should be between $ 215 as well as $ 210 when expiration happens within two months. When the cost is above $ 215 or perhaps under $ 210, the trader might nevertheless come up with a lessened income, but may also drop some money.

The damage becomes bigger in case the price tag of Apple stock approaches the top call strike ($220) or maybe the reduced put strike ($ 205). The maximum loss happens if the selling price of the stock trades previously $ 220 or under $205.

Believe the inventory at expiration is $ 225. This's above the top of the call strike price, which suggests the trader is dealing with the maximum possible loss. The sold call is losing $10 ($ 225 - $ 215), while the purchased call is producing $5 ($ 225 - $ 220). The places expire. The trader will lose $5, and $ 500 comprehensive (hundred share contracts), though they additionally got $ 396 in premiums. Thus, the damage is capped at $400 plus commissions.

Right now, think the cost of Apple rather fallen, however, not under the lower put threshold. It falls to $ 208. The quite short call is losing $ 2($ 208 - $ 210), or perhaps $ 200, while the long put expires useless. The calls likewise expire. The trader will lose $ 200 on the position but received $ 396 in premium credits. Thus, they nevertheless make $ 196, fewer commission expenses.

Chapter 7

SELLING NAKED OPTIONS

7.1 What's a Naked Option?

A naked choice, likewise referred to as an "uncovered" option, is produced once the seller of an option agreement doesn't wear the main security required to satisfy the possible obligation which results from the offering (also referred to as "writing" or maybe "shorting") an option. Offering a function generates an obligation of the seller to present an opportunity customer with the basic shares or maybe futures agreement for any corresponding lengthy position (for a call option) or maybe the money needed for a corresponding brief position (for a put choice) at expiration. In case the seller does not have any ownership of the underlying asset or maybe the corresponding funds needed for delivery of a put option. The seller will have to get it at expiration based on existing industry prices. With no protection out of the cost volatility, such roles are believed to be extremely susceptible to damage and therefore called uncovered, or even more colloquially, as naked.

7.2 Key elements

• Naked choices refer to an option sold with no previously set aside shares or maybe cash to satisfy the possibility of obligation at expiration.

• Naked options run the Risk of big loss from fast cost change before expiration.

• Naked call option, which is exercised, develop a brief placement in the seller's account.

• Naked put choices which are exercised build an extended position in the seller's account, bought with cash that is available.

7.3 The way a Naked Option Works

A naked job describes a circumstance where a trader offers a choice agreement without having a position in the underlying protection as shelter from an unwanted shift of cost. Naked choices are appealing to investors and traders since they have the expected volatility included in the price. In case the basic security movements in the exact opposite direction that the choice customer anticipated, or perhaps even when it moves in the buyer 's favor although not adequate to account because of the volatility pretty much built into the cost, then the seller of the possibility gets to keep some out of the cash premium. Which usually would mean that option sellers win about seventy % of trades? A setup which appeals to investors and traders who love to win the vast majority of the trades of theirs.

7.4 Naked Calls

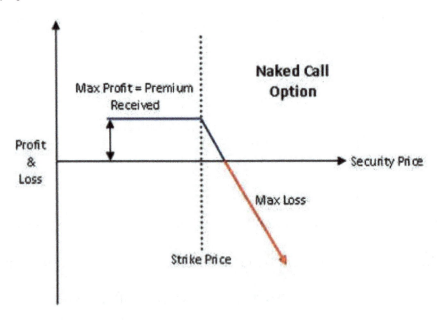

A trader that creates a naked call option on a stock has recognized the obligation to promote the basic stock for the strike cost at or even before expiration, no matter exactly how high the share priced rises. In case the trader doesn't wear the main stock, the seller is going to have to get the inventory, now provide the inventory to the choice customer to fulfill the obligation when the choice is exercised. The best outcome is the fact that this produces a short sell placement in the choice sellers accounts on the Monday after expiration. In the situation of a seller that sold a put option, the best outcome will be creating a great deal of inventory place in the possibility sellers account--a place bought with money out of the choice sellers account.

For instance, imagine a trader that thinks that a stock is not likely to rise in value with the following three months, though she's not so certain that a possible decline will be huge. Believe that the inventory is valued at $100, along with a $500 strike call, with an expiration date ninety many days in the long term, is being offered for $ 4.75 a share. She decides to start a naked call by "selling to open" those calls and gathering the premium. In this particular situation, she chooses not to buy the inventory since she thinks the possibility is apt to expire worthlessly, and she is going to keep the whole premium.

7.5 The possible three outcomes that are possible for a naked call trade:

Outcome #1: The stock rallies before expiration.

In this particular situation, the trader has a function that will be exercised. When we believe the stock rose to $ 130 on good earnings news, then the choice is going to be worked out at $100 a share. It means that the trader should acquire the inventory in the present market price, after which promote it (or short the inventory) from $100 a share to coat the obligation of her. These conditions lead to a $30 per share loss ($100- $ 130). There's no upper limit for just how high the inventory (and the choice seller's obligations) can rise.

Outcome #2: The stock stays dull near $500 per share at expiration. In case the inventory is at or perhaps below the strike price at expiration, it will not be worked out, and also, the option seller gets to hold the high quality she initially collected.

Outcome #3: The stock has dropped to the cost below $500 at expiration.

In this particular scenario, assume the stock dropped to $90 by expiration. Generally, there will not be some customers ready to spend the strike price ($500) for a stock they can purchase on the open market for $90 a share. As in result #2, the choice has no value as well as the choice seller gets to have the whole premium.

7.4 Naked Puts

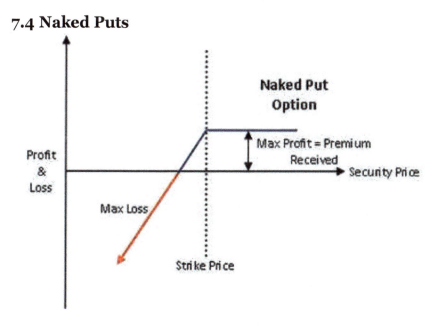

As you have seen it in the preceding results, there's simply no limit to just how tall an inventory can increase; therefore, a naked call seller has theoretically limitless threat. With naked puts, on the opposite hand, seller's danger is found because a stock, or maybe some other underlying asset, may just fall to 0 dollars. A naked put feature seller has recognized the obligation to purchase the underlying asset in the strike cost in case the choice is exercised at or even before the expiration date of its. Even though the danger is contained, it can still be pretty large; therefore, brokers normally have particular rules concerning naked choice trading. New traders, for instance, might not be allowed to put this order type.

Chapter 8

Roll Out OPTION

Rolling a trade is one of the ways to manage a winning or even losing position. To come to a swap, we simultaneously near our current place and start a brand new body. We can alter the strike, period, or perhaps both. With tastytrade, we look at rolling as a protective strategy as well as a roll for length to "keep the fantasy alive." We'll only roll if the assumption of ours is also the same. If the assumption of ours has changed, we appear to close the position of ours, or maybe leave defined chance spreads open and allow the probabilities play out. Knowing when you should come a trade may be subjective, though we look at several different facets of the trade to assist us in determining.

If the probability of ours of Profit is under 33 % and if the trade went past a person to 2 times the profit target of ours, we are going to look to come for the duration. We don't double the Risk of ours by doubling the contracts of ours; we just roll for the duration and a little credit. We like rolling for credit since it adds to the original profit potential of ours and extends the breakeven price of ours.

In the majority of cases, we don't look to roll defined chance trades. Whenever we go into the swap, we're at ease with the max damage, which can happen as well as enable the probabilities to play out. Nevertheless, in case we're "on the dance floor," along with the short strike of ours is somewhat ATM or ITM, and the long strike of ours is OTM, we might roll for the duration. Our scientific studies indicate that in case the assumption of ours will be the same as well as the basic is cyclical, we can roll constantly before we're correct and also make an income regularly.

8.1 Roll Out

"Rolling out" implies that an expiring feature job has been replaced with an identical trade in a later on options series. For instance, you may sell to close a January fifty call, and instantly purchase opening a March fifty calls.

You will find two scenarios where it is practical to roll out. In the very first, you have pinpointed a winning choice technique, and you feel sure the directional action will continue playing out in favor of yours. By taking earnings on the shorter-term trade and also simultaneously initiating the longer-term trade, you are positioned to maintain gaining from an extended action in favor of yours.

In the next, you will always feel positive in the original prediction of yours for the inventory -- though you have resolved that much more time is needed for the swap to play out when you expect. In this particular instance, you are purchasing more hours for the shares to meet the expectations of yours.

In both instances, rolling out must be approached with extreme caution. Under the very first situation, be sure the outlook for the stock will continue to help the trade thesis of yours, which you are not merely getting piggish after a great winner. In the next example, once again -- reexamine the rationale of yours for the trade. Does the stock just need a few weeks to move in favor of yours, or could it be time to admit that the initial analysis of yours might have been off-base?

Chapter 9

COMMON OPTIONS TRADING MISTAKES TO AVOID

Typical options trading mistakes to stay away from As a brand new choices trader, it's very common to feel overwhelmed. Among the advantages of trading options is it offers you an assortment of methods to make use of everything you think might happen to the main security. But among the trade-offs for the luxury of the range is a heightened risk to make mistakes. The aim of this is to let you know about several of the most typical choices trading mistakes to be able to help choices traders make much more informed decisions.

Mistake #1: The strategy does not match the outlook of yours.

A crucial component when starting to trade options is the capability to build an outlook for everything you believe could happen. Two of the typical starting points for developing a perspective are using technical analysis as well as fundamental analysis, or maybe a mix of both. The complex analysis involves interpreting industry action (mainly price and volume) on a chart and also searching for areas of assistance, resistance, or trends to be able to determine possible buy/sell potentials. The essential analysis includes reviewing a company 's economical statements, performance data, along with existing company fashion to produce an outlook on airers4you 's price. An outlook not just includes a directional bias, although it entails a time frame for the length of time you think the idea of yours is going to take to do the job.

As you review various alternatives methods, it's essential to ensure that the technique you select is created to make use of the perspective you expect. Fidelity's Options Strategy Guide is a proven way to understand strategies that are different, and also could enable you to figure out the best 1 for the situation of yours.

Mistake #2: Choosing the incorrect expiration

With strategies, you're confronted with the problem associated with a wide range of options when choosing an expiration date. The best part is the fact that in case you create an outlook, then choosing the appropriate expiration typically falls into place. One way to enable you to pick the best expiration for the outlook of yours is having an easy checklist:

- Just how long do I think it is going to take because of the swap to play out?
- Do I wish to store the swap via an earnings announcement, stock split, or maybe several other situations?
- Can there be sufficient liquidity to allow for the trade of mine?

Mistake #3:

Choosing the incorrect placement size

Most position sizing mistakes stem from two typical emotions: greed or fear. In case you're greedy when making choices, you can wind up trading a position color, which is simply too large for the account size of yours. This might occur if a trade goes contrary to the outlook, and afterward, you are bound to a crippling loss. On the flip side, you might be as some traders who trade incredibly little. Trading a little size is fine, though you might miss out on a substance return.

Typical means of position sizing include:

Risk a portion of your account value on 1 %, 3 %, 2 %, etc. Make use of a regular dollar value $100, $1,000, $500, etc.

Ultimately, when picking out the trade size, you need to be at ease with the quantity of capital you are going to lose if the trade does not go in favor of yours. Preferably, the trade size must be big enough to be significant to the bank account, but sufficiently small so you do not lose sleep during the night.

Mistake #4:

Ignoring volatility

Implied volatility is a degree of exactly what the industry expects volatility to have the world for a certain security. It's crucial to tell if implied volatility is pretty high or even low since it can help identify the cost of an opportunity premium. Knowing whether the premium is costly or cheap is a crucial factor when choosing what option strategy makes probably the most sense for the outlook of yours. In case the choices are fairly inexpensive, it could be advisable to look at debit methods, whereas when the choices are fairly costly, you might be much better served looking for credit methods.

Mistake #5:

Not using likelihood considering the probabilities for the strategy of yours is a crucial element when choosing to put a trade. Not merely will it place into perspective what's statistically apt to occur, though it's crucial to understanding whether your risk/reward seems sensible. You must be aware that probability does not have a directional bias. It's merely the statistical possibility of the cost being at a specific level on the evaluation date, provided the present elements. You can make use of Fidelity's Probability Calculator (provided by Dash Financial Technologies LLC) to help you make the determination.

To us, the picture above, think about this particular example of an 1140/1150 put credit spread and just how probabilities can play into the evaluation. The likelihood of cost being previously 1150 at expiration is about 68 % and has around a 77 % chance of getting under 1140. At expiration, any cost more than 1150 represents optimum gain, so any cost below 1140 presents a maximum loss. In case you are merely in a position to gather $2.50 for your $10 spread, and then simply looking at the probabilities by itself, you can see if you're getting compensated for the chance.

68 % of the precious time you are going to obtain the optimum benefit of $ 250 $ 250 x 0.68 = $ 170

27 % of the precious time you are going to realize the optimum damage of $ 750 $ 750 x 0.27 = $ 202.50

If perhaps you total the two quantities outside, there's a net loss of $32.50. What this means is when you constantly place yourself in this particular situation, the probabilities dictate with the time you must have damaging return shipping, statistically speaking. Remember 5 % of the precious time, the underlying cost in this particular instance is going to fall between max gain as well as max loss, as well as the gain or maybe loss on the position may vary, which will influence the total loss computation negatively or positively.

Mistake #6: Focusing on the expiration graph As being a trader, it's essential to always assess the quantity of risk/reward you've on the dinner table as well as check to find out if it also makes good sense for the account of yours. Entirely concentrating on the positions expiration graph of yours does not tell just how many risks you transport these days, or perhaps on a future date.

The light blue line symbolizes the role at expiration; the white line represents position these days, so the yellow line is a date selected in the long term. In this particular example, the vertical white-colored line has been moved to the present market price of the main, and exactly where it intersects with such lines tells just how much loss or profit for the trade.

As the placement stands in this particular example, you have received the vast majority of income and also have a considerable quantity of space on the drawback to recognize optimum loss come expiration when the placement moves against you. At this time, you might think about, will be the possible downside danger worth always keeping the position on to understand the maximum gain?

You might think about what would happen when the position makes a big move in either direction with the ensuing days. If it can make a move up, you would keep on making extra revenue, though it will be a nominal amount concerning what you have made. On the opposite side, with a big downward move, you might lose a major component of the profits you have made. At this time in the swap, the risk/reward has altered and will go unnoticed in case you concentrate just on the expiration day.

Mistake #7: Not working with a trading strategy

One of the very first stages in staying away from typical trading mistakes is having a good trading plan. A simple trading plan must consist have, however, not been limited to:

- Just how much do you think you're prepared to risk per trade?

- How would you discover opportunities in the market place?

- When are you going to go into the industry?

- What's the exit strategy of yours?

As stated, greed, fear, and before can result in irrational decisions that you would not ordinarily make. The primary advantage of working with a trading plan is removing these psychological feelings from the Trading of yours. Additionally, it creates a method that is very easily repeatable. Repeatability is a crucial element that will help you learn from mistakes and also have the capability to obtain flaws in the trades you set. Without having a scheme, it gets really hard to boost as a trader &; continue to move forward.

Chapter 10

THE OPTION TRADER MINDSET

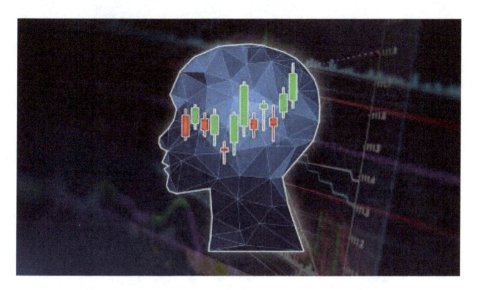

Options are among the most flexible instruments in the monetary markets. The flexibility of theirs enables the trader to leverage the position of theirs to boost returns. These items likewise enable the person to control Risk through the use of them for hedging or perhaps to generate an income out of the benefit, downside, and sideways action of the marketplace.

Even with the many benefits of its, options trading carries a substantial threat of damage, and also it's speculative. Not everybody could become a booming choices trader. Like every additional business, getting a profitable choices trader demands a particular set of skills, character type, and mindset.

1. Have the ability to Manage Risk

Choices are high-risk instruments, and also traders must realize just how much danger they've at any point in time. What's the optimum downside of the swap? What's the explicit or implicit place concerning volatility? Just how much of the capital of mine is allocated towards the trade? These are several of the questions traders often have to keep in the minds theirs.

Traders also have to take proper steps to control Risk. Particularly, if you're a short term options trader, you'll frequently run into loss-making trades. For instance, in case you keep a position overnight, the bet of yours may go bad due to adverse news. You have to have the ability to minimize the danger of the positions of yours at any time. Many traders do so by restricting the trade size of theirs and diversifying into many different trades, so all the eggs of theirs are not in the same bin.

An options trader additionally needs to be a great money manager. They have to use the capital theirs wisely. For instance, it would not be a good idea to block 90 % of the capital of yours in one trade. Whatever technique you adopt, risk management, as well as cash management, can't be dismissed.

2. Be good With Numbers

While Trading of options, you're constantly dealing with numbers. What is the implied volatility? Will be the Option in cash or from the money? What is the break, even of the trade? Choices traders will always be answering these questions. Additionally, they talk about options Greeks, like the delta, vega, gamma, and theta of the options trades of theirs. For instance, a trader would wish to find out whether the trade of his is short gamma.

3. Have Discipline

To become successful, options traders should practice discipline. Doing considerable investigation, identifying options, creating the proper industry, sticking and forming to a method, creating objectives, and developing an exit strategy is part of the discipline. A basic illustration of deviating from the discipline is sticking to the herd. Never trust a viewpoint without having done your research of yours. You cannot skip the homework of yours as well as blame the herd for the losses of yours. Rather, you have to devise an unbiased trading strategy that works for it to be a booming options strategy.

While proper education in the type of higher degrees may be connected with the best traders, it's not always the case for those. Though you should be educated about the industry, profitable traders take time to understand the basic principles and examine the market - different scenarios, various trends - everything and anything about the way the market will work. They're not typically novices that have taken a three-hour trading seminar on "How getting rich quick trading," but only take the time to find out through the marketplace.

4. Be Patient

Patience is a quality all options traders have. Patient investors are ready to hold out for the marketplace to offer the proper opportunity instead of attempting to make a huge win on every industry movement. You'll usually notice traders sitting idle and seeing the industry, waiting for the best time to enter and exit a trade. The same isn't the situation with amateur traders. They're impatient, not able to manage the emotions of theirs, and they are going to be fast to get into and exit trades.

6. Develop a Trading Style

Each trader boasts a unique personality and must adopt a trading style that suits him or maybe the traits of her. Many traders might be great at day trading, wherever they purchase as well as market c option a few times throughout the day for making little earnings. Many might be far more at ease with position trading, wherever they develop trading techniques to make use of special opportunities, like time decay and volatility. And some could be far more at ease with swing trading, in which traders generate bets on the price movement over a specific periods lasting five to thirty times.

7. Interpret the News

Traders need to have the ability to understand the news, sort hype from the truth, and make proper choices based on this understanding. You are going to find numerous traders willing to throw the capital of theirs in an option with promising news, and the following day they'll start working on the subsequent big news. This distracts them from determining even bigger trends on the market. Many effective traders are going to be truthful with them and make good personal choices, instead of simply going by the best stories in the media.

7.be an energetic Learner

The Chicago Board of Trade (CBOT) reported 90 % of choices traders would recognize losses. What separates effective traders from typical people is effective traders are in a position to learn from the losses of theirs and implement what they discover in the trading strategies of theirs. Best traders practice...and train several much more before they discover the lessons behind the industry understand the economics behind the marketplace and also watch the marketplace conduct as its occurring.

The financial markets are continuously changing as well as evolving; you have to have a clear knowledge of what is happening and just how everything works. By turning into an active learner, you won't just be great at the current trading strategies of yours. However, you'll additionally have the ability to determine brand new possibilities others may not see or even could pass over.

8. Be Flexible

You can't stake a claim on the market but should opt for the marketplace or even escape it when it's not the kind that fits you. You have to accept losses occur, and it's unavoidable that you'll lose. Acceptance instead of fighting the industry is paramount to understanding, transparency as well as lastly winning.

9. Plan the Trades of yours

An option trader that has plans is much more apt to achieve success than one that operates on feeling and instinct. When you do not have a scheme, you are going to place arbitrary trades, and so, you will be directionless. On the flip side, in case you have a scheme, you're far more apt to stick with it. You are going to be clear about what the goals of yours are and just how you intend to achieve them. You'll likewise understand how to cover the losses of yours or even when to book earnings. You can find out how the program has worked (or not worked) for you. These steps are vital to creating a strong trading method.

10. Keep Records

Best options traders keep conscientious records of the trades of theirs. Maintaining suitable trade records is a crucial habit that will help you stay away from making costly decisions. The reputation of your trade records additionally provides insightful info to allow you to boost the odds of yours of success.

Chapter 11

Trading with leaps

How do you want to make use of the long-term investment advantages provided by stocks at a reduced price? In that case, then think about investing in the LEAP option.

LEAP choices (or LEAPs) are feature contracts that expire one period out of the day of purchase. The acronym LEAP stands for "Long term Equity Anticipation."

LEAPs are much more inexpensive compared to stocks since they are offered for option contract prices. They are long-range investments, so that they provide you with lots of time to make use of stock price moves without the high-cost of the underlying securities.

In this book, we will go over LEAP options so that you can determine if you have got far in the trading strategy of yours. To play the Long Game, Many traders frequently purchase or even sell choices that expire in the following month. Although that type of a method can offer several substantial returns, additionally, it provides the underlying stock hardly any time to move up or even down.

LEAP option solves the problem and has a contract expiration that is a minimum of a year through. The stock has an extended time to stay within the trend line you predicted and drive out daily cost swings.

Regrettably, Leaps costlier compared to short term contracts for exactly that reason. You will pay a premium once you purchase LEAPs.

That should not matter whether the stock moves in the correct direction. The cost of the possible contract must increase accordingly.

In case you are new to the word "the Greeks," it describes a pair of statistics about any feature contract. Those statistics are diagnosed with Greek letters.

Key in on two Greeks, particularly when purchasing LEAP options: **delta** and **theta.**

Theta methods time decay. The better a functioning agreement receives to expiration, the more it will lose value. That is particularly true in case it is out of the investment.

Keep in mind: **theta** additionally speeds up when the agreement gets even closer to expiration. Put simply, the daily time decay throughout the final week of the agreement will surpass the day-to-day time decay whenever the agreement still has weeks before expiration.

That is why theta will not affect LEAPs that a lot initially. Nevertheless, time decay is going to become painfully apparent as the agreement gets even closer to expiration.

Bottom line: it is a terrific idea to purchase LEAP options which are prone to a spike in value properly before expiration. The way, you will not need to be concerned much about theta.

The options Greek, **delta,** is the actual one you need to check out carefully before purchasing a LEAP.

Why? Because it measures just how much the cost of the possibility swings concerning the cost of the underlying stock.

A delta of, 80, for instance, implies the choice cost is going to rise eighty cents for each dollar that the stock priced rises.

If you purchase LEAPs, search for options with good deltas. The way, the investment of yours is going to increase in value on a nearly dollar-for-dollar time frame with the underlying stock.

Must you purchase out-of-the-money or in-the-money LEAPs? Just as before, it depends.

In case you have not had familiarity with the phrases "in-the-money" as well as "out-of-the-money," they talk about the cost of the basic stock concerning the possibility contract's strike selling price.

Call choices are in the cash whenever the strike price is under the stock price and from the cash when the strike price is much more than the stock price.

Put choices are in the cash whenever the strike price is much more than the stock price and from the cash when the strike price is under the stock price.

If you are right into a speculative trade, be at liberty to purchase out-of-the-money LEAP options. Simply remember that you will spend a hefty premium when compared with short term contracts as well as the basic stock may have to advance the way of yours considerably before you visit a good return.

As a general guideline, in-the-money choices have larger deltas. That is why they are a wonderful option for LEAPs.

Naturally, in-the-money options are costlier compared to out-of-the-money options because they have previously "arrived." But options that are not far in cash continue to be a lot cheaper compared to the underlying stock.

Real-Life Example Utilizing a LEAP Option

We need to say Apple is trading at $175 a share. You believe it is going up considerably over the very long term; therefore, you choose to purchase a LEAP option.

The $170 call option for 12 months out is now trading for $24.00. You think Apple is increasing a minimum of thirty dollars per share before the contract expires, which means you feel it's got potential.

You take a look at the Greeks. The contract carries a delta of 0.63. Which means for each dollar that Apple stock increases in value, the choice will boost sixty-three cents? That is acceptable since additionally, you know that delta is going to increase when the stock price increases.

The theta is 0.04. That means the choice is going to lose four cents in value each day, other things being equal. That is also appropriate.

You purchase the call option for $44. That suggests you invest $2,400 since choices are purchased in blocks of hundred shares (Trading with leaps 24*100= Trading with leaps 2,400).

Sure enough, after several months or more, Apple reports the stock and record earnings price shoots up to Trading with leaps $198 a share. The option you bought is now currently worth $41 trading with leaps you sell the position for Trading with leaps for $ 4,100 (Trading with leaps

41x 100).That means the return of yours is a whopping 70 %!

Today compare that to what you would get if you bought 100 shares of stock. You would pay $ 17,500 ($175 x 100) for the position and sell the inventory for $19,800 ($198 x hundred). That is going to provide you with a return of only 13 %.

Therefore in case you bought the stock, you would invest a great deal more money for a significantly smaller return.

That is part of the reason that makes LEAP choices appealing to a lot of traders.

Conclusion

Trading options involves a selection of considerations both before as well as after the trade have been placed. A lot of the mistakes mentioned may be accounted for before the trade is opened through the use of the tools as well as materials Fidelity offers. The one most significant step to trading options is developing a scheme as well as stick with it! Several of the equipment, as well as materials that will help you build your own plan of yours, are the Options Strategy Guide, Probability Calculator, Key Statistics, moreover the Profit/Loss Calculator. Make use of these along with other trading programs and resources Fidelity offers to allow you to stay away from these typical choices trading mistakes in the future trades of yours.

CPSIA information can be obtained
at www.ICGtesting.com
Printed in the USA
LVHW011330210121
676966LV00005B/250

9 781801 442466